Professional

Website Secret

Hosting, Training, Live Support!

P.J. Germain

Disclaimer

This book has been written for information purposes only. Every effort has been made to make this book as complete and accurate as possible. However, there may be mistakes in typography or content. Also, this e-book provides information only up to the publishing date. Therefore, this book should be used as a guide - not as the ultimate source.

The purpose of this book is to educate. The author and the publisher does not warrant that the information contained in this book is fully complete and shall not be responsible for any errors or omissions. The author and publisher shall have neither liability nor responsibility to any person or entity with respect to any loss or damage caused or alleged to be caused directly or indirectly by this book.

About the Author

 P.j. Germain is an author, engineer, entrepreneur, certified webmaster, successful Affiliate Marketing and SEO Coach living in Pensacola, FL who loves sharing knowledge and helping others build a successful online business.

After attempting many online businesses and spending thousands of dollars, P.j. has finally discovered the secret to building online success absolutely free of charge. After years of testing and development, he has put together this resource to help guide others on the path to financial freedom.

P.j. has a reputation for honesty and integrity and is a passionate person who will go the extra mile and over-deliver.

P.j.'s words of wisdom:

"I believe that knowledge is power. Everyone should improve themselves and/or business, no matter what stage of life they're in. Whether it's to develop a better mindset or to increase profits. Moving forward, one step at a time is the key. Life is an adventure. Live each and cherish each moment."

If you would like to learn more from P.j., please visit:

http://PureResiduals.com

Table of Contents

Introduction And What You Will Learn

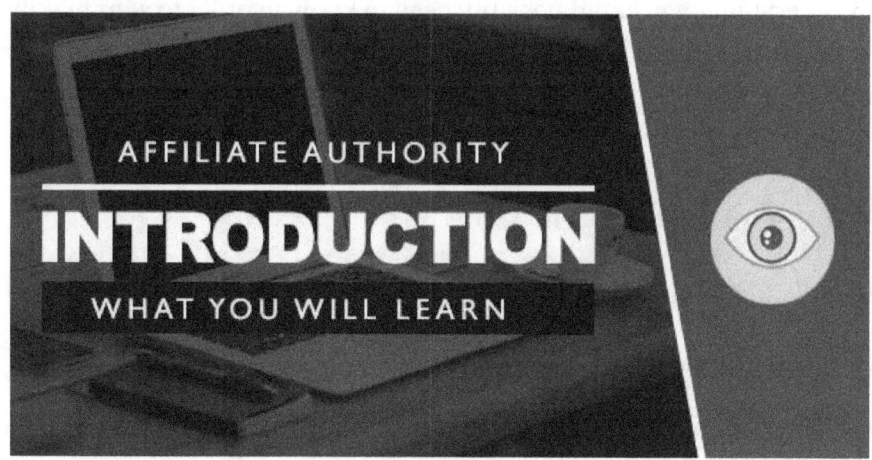

Using affiliate marketing it's possible to make a small or even big fortune with zero up-front investment, zero creative process and zero marketable skills. This might sound too good to be true but in fact there are plenty of examples of precisely this happening. Look up affiliate marketing online and you'll find a whole culture of people who have private jets and yachts, who travel around the world and who have almost celebrity like status online.

And this isn't a rarity. Affiliate marketing is a process that is highly repeatable – there's a *blueprint* for using it and it can reliably earn you big money *every time*.

So the big question is: why isn't *everybody* doing it?

The answer is simply that most people don't know about it. And even when they do hear of it, they often find it too daunting sounding and too unbelievable to even try it.

That's good news for *us* because it means there are still products and buyers out there for us to make money from.

1

And the other good news? You have this book! And this book will tell you everything you could possibly need to know in order to start making *huge* profits from affiliate marketing. This book will make *you* into that affiliate marketing authority and will help you to generate passive income on a huge scale – all by selling other people's products!

What You Will Learn

Specifically then, throughout the course of this book, you will learn:

- What affiliate marketing is and how it works

- Why affiliate marketing is one of the best ways to generate revenue online

- The different types of affiliate network

- How to choose the best affiliate network and product for you

- How to sign up and get started as a sellerHow to create a landing page for your affiliate products

- How to use PPC advertising to drive traffic to your landing page

- How to create ads that get clicked and that offer great ROI

- How to build a mailing list

- How to use content marketing to become an authority in your niche

- How to use social media to grow your prominence online

- How to write persuasive text that encourages sales

- How to grow your affiliate marketing business

- The Professional Website Secret where you can do it all with ZERO investment – Absolutely no money needed (upfront or ever)

Why Affiliate Marketing?
The Facts And Figures You Need To Know

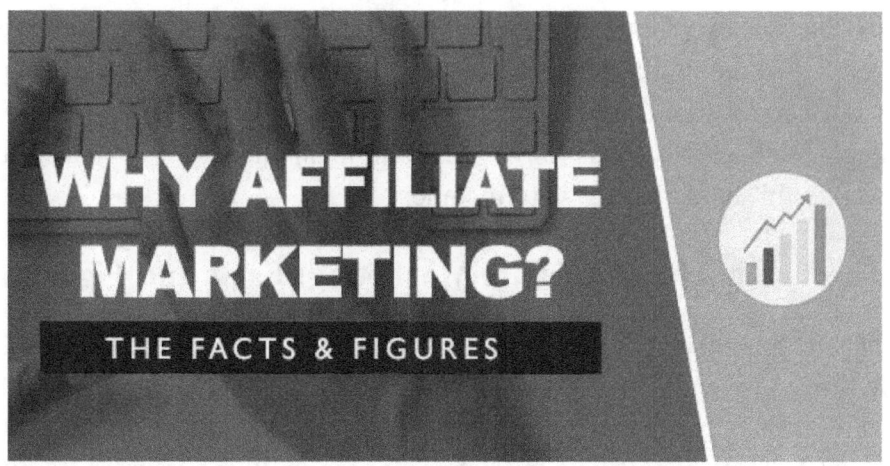

To begin with then, what precisely *is* affiliate marketing?

Simply put, affiliate marketing means marketing as an affiliate. This basically means selling products in order to get commission – just as you might do as a door-to-door salesman for cable TV.

Of course the life of a door-to-door salesman is a rather unpleasant one because they're travelling around all day, getting doors slammed in their face and only earning money if they get fortunate enough to land a sale. As a salesman you live and die by your ability to persuade a cynical audience and you invest huge amounts of time to try and make the sale.

As an online affiliate things are a little different. Now you'll be selling products for commission but you'll be doing it through the web and you'll be letting your customers come to you. You'll have any means necessary available to you to achieve this with and you'll be able to constantly tweak and improve the system you're using to make sales. What's more, you can learn from the advice and mistakes of others and in some cases even use templates. In fact, you can even *outsource* the marketing process!

And because you're investing less time in marketing this way, you can take on as many different products as you want and thereby scale up your income significantly. Moreover, you can do this 'on the side' to begin with and not rely on it for your main income – it makes a wonderful supplement to your income.

The Truth About Affiliate Marketing: Facts and Figures

That's affiliate marketing in a nutshell but what do the numbers say?

Affiliate marketing has certainly been growing over the years with about 5.7% of big affiliate marketers starting in 2006 versus 13.9% in 2012. Most affiliate marketers are between 31-40 according to surveys and target B2C products (business to consumer) rather than B2B (business to business). 91% of these affiliate marketers choose e-mail marketing as their primary method of contacting customers while 60% work from home.

What's really interesting though is the salary. While nearly 40% of affiliate marketers earned below $5K in 2013 and use it as a secondary source of income, the top earners surveyed earned as much as $500K (this accounted for 3.3% of marketers). 50% were earning *at least* $10K a year, whereas about 20% were on $50K+. Not bad! (Data from Three Ladders Marketing).

More data from Webprom shows us that UK businesses earned 14 billion GBP in 2013. This was up 15% from 2012, showing more growth still.

The bottom line? Digital marketing is a highly lucrative job that appeals particularly to young entrepreneurs. There's a lot of money to be made and the industry is only growing with time.

Affiliate Marketing vs Selling a Product

If there's a downside to affiliate marketing, it's that you won't keep 100% of the profits you generate – which can be disheartening. The percentages you get for affiliate marketing actually are very good and in some cases you get more of the profit than the creator – a lot of suggest that creators and producers give their affiliates 60% of the income as the *starting point* in fact. And it's unusual to see affiliate marketing get you much less than 40%.

But then again, this still isn't *100%*. So now the question becomes, why would you choose to use affiliate marketing when you *could* be getting all the profit by creating and selling your own product?

There are many answers but the first is that you don't have to go through the lengthy process of creating a product to sell. The sorts of things that sell very well online are quite often digital products – which means e-books, online courses and software. Any of these things take a lot of time to create and a lot of skill – if you're not a proficient writer, then you might struggle to create an e-book that people are going to be happy to pay for. Likewise, if you're not a programmer, you probably can't make the next must-have piece of software. And if it's a physical product you want to sell, you'll have to learn the entire manufacturing process.

Now you have two options. One is to *learn* the necessary skills or just to work hard to overcome your limitations. You might write and rewrite your e-book for instance, get it proofread and then rewrite it again. But it will be a slow process. You could learn to code meanwhile, or you could learn how products are designed and created.

The other option is to outsource the entire process. If you can't write/program/design, then you can find someone who *can* by going onto a site like UpWork, Elance or People Per Hour. So is this a good strategy? Well yes, it can be, but it will also cost you a big upfront investment and it will mean you lose some control over the outcome. The best programmer in the world can make you an amazing piece of software but they can't read your mind – so that software may not be precisely how you imagined it. Likewise, a good writer will try to stick to your guidelines, but unless you give them a full-length draft they're always going to insert some of their own ideas and opinions which may be contrary to your own.

And here's the thing: you can never know if a product is going to be popular or not. So in other words, if you spend months and hundreds of dollars creating your product, you may yet find that there's no one interested in buying it. Of course this will then leave you at a huge loss and you'll have to either give up or sink even *more* money into yet another untested idea. It's actually quite a rough ride!

Smart business nous will tell you instead to use the 'fail fast' approach. This means testing as many ideas and products as you can to begin with to see what sticks and not committing yourself financially to any project unless you have *some* evidence that it's going to be successful. When you fail with affiliate marketing you lose nothing and you can thus keep trying different products until you find the one you'll profit from best.

And what's even better? You can pick a product that's *already* selling well and that's *already* getting amazing reviews. You can literally find someone online who is making a killing from selling an affiliate product and then you can sell *that exact same product* knowing that it's possible to get rich from that strategy. When you sell your own product and it's not making the money you hoped it would, you may find you can't tell whether it's the product or your sales strategy that is holding you back.

With affiliate marketing you know that the product works, so it's just a matter of finding the best way to peddle it.

Now there are scenarios where it *does* make more sense to create your own product and ultimately this gives you more freedom and flexibility and more profit. But for a lot of people, affiliate marketing makes more sense at least to begin with.

How Affiliate Marketing Works

Now you know why affiliate marketing is so appealing, it's time to look at how affiliate marketing works, both from a technical perspective and from a practical one.

Affiliate Marketing In Technical Terms

Essentially, affiliate marketing relies on cookies. Cookies are small files that you can store on the computer of any online web user. These cookies can then be used to identify that user at a later point or to retrieve information about them. Cookies are what enable sites like Facebook to keep you signed in for example and they can also be used by advertising companies to show you ads relevant to your browsing history.

In the case of affiliate marketing, cookies are used in order to show that traffic came from your website/advert and these work alongside unique 'identifier URLs' which are your private gateway to that website.

Affiliate Marketing In Layman's Terms

So in other words, you have your own address that you use to send people to the product page. They then get redirected to the main site but during the process a cookie is stored on their computer that is basically the digital equivalent of 'tell 'em I sent you'. Then, when they buy a product, this is logged in your profile and at the end of the week/month/quarter you get paid your due.

To get started in digital marketing then, all you need to do is to find a product you like and you think you can sell, sign up to the affiliate program and then paste your unique link in any form of marketing, advertising or otherwise. That could be a Facebook ad, it could be an e-mail or it could even be a physical flier.

We'll look into the details in subsequent chapters but that basically outlines how the process works.

Affiliate Marketers for Product Creators

While reading this you might find that your pupils have been replaced with dollar signs as you consider all the possibilities. Truly, the ability to profit from someone else's product is in many ways an ideal situation and especially when you know that product is a good seller and you're getting the lion's share of the profit!

But this might also have left you wondering why it is that someone would put their products up for sale this way and why they'd offer to give you most of the profit. What's in it for the product developer? Understanding this can help you to better understand how the whole system works and to make even better use of it.

So basically, when you let an affiliate sell your product, it means giving away profit. But at the same time, the first thing to realise is that they also aren't *losing* this profit. That's because they're still going to be able to sell the products themselves as well – so all the sales that you make for them are *extra*.

They can then market their product as much as they possibly can and earn 100% profit on all that hard work. But at the same time, they'll now *also* have more sales coming in from you. They might only get an extra 40% of those sales, but that's still 40% more than they would have gotten otherwise and it's *on top* of what they can otherwise earn.

Now if the product is popular, there's a good chance there will be more than one affiliate selling it. Thus you may have a situation where you're getting money from hundreds of people all promoting your product. And if one of them happens to be a real pro, they could conceivably bring in *thousands* of dollars on top of your usual profits.

This is obviously pretty awesome from the creator of that product and *that* is why they're happy to give away some of their profit and some of their control.

Also worth considering though is why some people *won't* offer affiliate programs for their products. More often than not, this is about control of the brand and reputation. If your sellers push too hard and are too forceful in their marketing, they can actually end up hurting your reputation and for this reason, you might choose to ensure that only you are allowed to sell your product.

When it goes well though, this is the ultimate 'win/win' situation and a truly symbiotic relationship. Find the right product and the right seller and you can both be rich!

How To Get Started With Affiliate Marketing

So now you understand the basics, how do you go about getting started and actually trying your hand at affiliate marketing?

The first thing you of course need to do is to find a product that you can sell as an affiliate. To do this, there are a few different approaches…

Top Affiliate Networks You Need To Know About

The main method through which to become an affiliate marketer is to start selling products from an affiliate network. Affiliate networks are basically online tools that make it easy for you to find products and to manage your sales and income. Affiliate networks give you access to popular products and they automate the entire process so that you don't have to communicate directly with the seller. They streamline the process in other words.

When it comes to choosing an affiliate network, there are three main choices. These are JVZoo, ClickBank and WSO Pro. We'll look at each of them in a little more detail below.

JVZoo
http://www.jvzoo.com/

JVZoo is arguably the best choice for the vast majority of affiliate marketers in the internet marketing space. This is because it is fast and simple to use with a highly intuitive interface and because it has a broad range of products to sell. It also has fairly low fees compared to some other choices.

This is a great choice for beginners and it's generally a good all-round choice.

ClickBank
http://www.clickbank.com

Very similar to JVZoo is ClickBank. ClickBank has been around longer than JVZoo and has a *huge* library of products and community of marketers. This stands in its favour and ensures that it remains one of the most popular choices for many marketers.

Categories

- ARTS & ENTERTAINMENT
- BETTING SYSTEMS
- BUSINESS / INVESTING
- COMPUTERS / INTERNET
- COOKING, FOOD & WINE
- E-BUSINESS & E-MARKETING
- EDUCATION
- EMPLOYMENT & JOBS
- FICTION
- GAMES
- GREEN PRODUCTS
- HEALTH & FITNESS
- HOME & GARDEN
- LANGUAGES
- MOBILE
- PARENTING & FAMILIES
- POLITICS / CURRENT EVENTS
- REFERENCE
- SELF-HELP
- SOFTWARE & SERVICES
- SPIRITUALITY, NEW AGE & ALTERNATIVE BELIEFS
- SPORTS
- TRAVEL

On the downside though, ClickBank is also a lot more complicated and fiddly to use and is in some ways very dated. It's enough to put a lot of people off using it and it isn't a good choice for absolute beginners for that reason. At the same time, ClickBank also has the highest fees.

With JVZoo available as an option, you might wonder why anyone would choose to use ClickBank. Of course it all comes down to the products – and if you can only find the product you really want to sell on ClickBank, then you'll have to make do with that setup. Just take a look at the broad range of categories you can browser:

WSO Prohttp://www.warriorforum.com/warrior-special-offers/ and https://warriorplus.com/wsopro/

The third option, WSO Pro, is a little different. WSO Pro stands for 'Warrior Special Offers' which is referring to the very well known and prolific 'Warrior Forum'. Warrior Forum is a forum specifically aimed at internet marketers and webmasters. This is where they come to discuss the best methods for gaining exposure, the best ways to build websites, the best tools for social media *etc*.

A lot of people sell products on this forum on the section called 'Warrior Special Offers' and they have the option to open the products up to affiliates as well.

WSO Pro is a great choice because the products are all created by other marketers who know exactly which kinds of things sell well and how to make sales. WSO Pro also has a very active community where you can share tips and see how other people are making money *and* it has the lowest fees of all three options.

But at the same time, WSO Pro also is the most limited in terms of the types of products you'll be selling. All these products are aimed squarely at internet marketers meaning they'll be e-books *on* making money online.

Other Networks

There are also many other networks for those that can't find what they're looking for on those three. Commission Junction was once one of the very biggest affiliate networks but was renamed to CJ Affiliate by Conservant a while back. They're one of the biggest networks but aren't a great choice for beginners being hard to get approved and being quite complex.

DigiResults is another interesting choice that is somewhat smaller than the others we've looked at but has the advantage of paying out immediately (yes immediately!) into your PayPal account. It's very

flexible and free but doesn't have quite the same wealth of products to pick from.

Affiliate Networks vs Other Options

One criticism against affiliate networks and affiliate schemes is that they very often tend to focus on the digital marketing niche more than any other. Browse through ClickBank, WSO Pro or JVZoo and you'll find that the majority of what's there falls into this category.

That's fine to an extent but it does limit your niche choices somewhat and it also means that this particular market is one that is *very* saturated. There are a billion e-books on making money online and there are a billion different people selling them. Your challenge here is to find a way to stand out.

If you want a broader range of products to sell then, you might choose to look to other options as an affiliate marketer. Here you have a few:

Finding Products Online

One option is simply to find products online and this will open you up considerably in terms of the types of products you end up selling. Take a look on the web for protein shakes, for orthotic shoes, for diabetes treatments and you will find that many of them have the option to 'become an affiliate' listed right down the bottom. Now all you need to do is sign up through their site and again start selling in the exact same way with your own link.

The same also goes for a lot of services. Gambling sites, stock brokers and more will often offer you commission on referrals and the best part of this is that often this commission is for the lifetime of that membership. What this means, is that if someone signs up to a binary broker online using your referral link, you'll then get a percentage of *all*

16

the profit they make subsequently. This means you can feasibly stop marketing completely eventually and still be making a huge profit while you sleep… forever!

The problem with finding affiliate products this way is that you're relying entirely on the goodwill of the manufacturer with no intervening third party. At the same time, you'll generally get much lower commission. If you find shoes to sell online you probably *won't* get 30% of every sale – apart from anything else they have much higher overheads themselves to account for.

And of course, you might also decide to try and promote a product that doesn't have an existing affiliate program at all. In other words, if you find someone selling an e-book, a piece of software or a product that you really love, then you can just get in contact with them via e-mail and ask them if they'd consider letting you sell it for them. This way you can also negotiate the terms of your own deal.

The upshot of this is that you get complete control over what you sell and you don't have to agree to a deal that won't work for you. On the other hand though, it also means you need to find a seller who is open to ideas and you never know what they're going to be like to work with until you really get stuck in!

Amazon

Another way to be an affiliate online is to sell Amazon products. Amazon has an affiliate system where you can sell their products on your site and get commission. This of course gives you access to millions of different products which you will find makes it much easier to fit your selling in with your existing online presence. If you have a fitness site, now you can sell dumbbells and running shoes. Likewise, if you have a website about computer games, you can sell all the games that you're recommending directly.

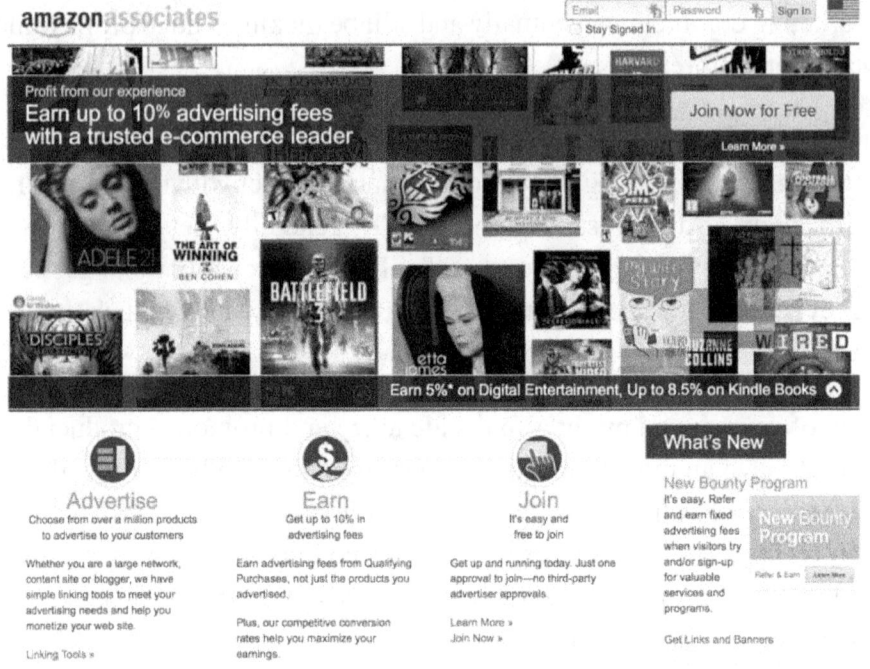

Amazon also has lots of great tools to make it easier to sell your products and to manage your sales. *But* it also doesn't give you very much commission... *at all*. When selling products on Amazon, expect to get commission of about 4%. This is pretty low indeed and it means you can sell a *lot* of games, books, DVDs and protein shakes and still come away with just a few dollars to show for it. In short then, you need to carefully consider which setup is best for you.

How To Choose a Product To Promote And What To Look For

Once you've chosen your network, or you've decided *not* to go with a network, the next thing to do is to pick your product.

There are several considerations here to think about and the best choice will ultimately depend on your goals and your current situation. Read below to get some ideas…

Your Current Audience

If you're reading this, then there's a good chance that you are already some kind of internet marketer/entrepreneur. In that case, there's a good chance you already have a website or blog, a mailing list or generally some form of direct audience that you can sell to. And as such, it of course makes a lot of sense to try and choose a product that will work for your existing audience. In other words, pick something in the niche you're already in, whether that be fitness, dating, making money or something else entirely.

Conversion Rates, EPC, Gravity And Other Stats

Easily the best way to determine whether a product is worth promoting is to take a look at its product sales stats.

I will show you what to look for and how to read certain stats before promoting a product. This essential skill should help you with most affiliate programs.

JVZoo

You'll now be able to search and browse products:

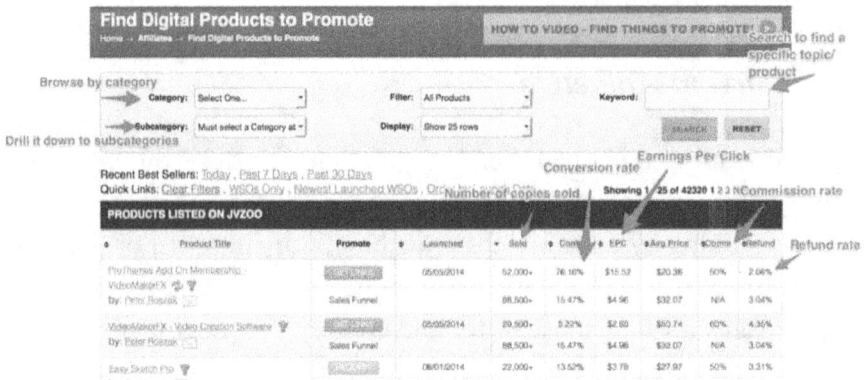

Factors to look for:

Number of copies sold. Usually a product that has sold a lot means it is in demand.

Conversion rate. You definitely want to be looking at conversion rate as it will determine whether your visitors will turn into customers.

EPC. Earnings Per Click is the average earnings you will get per click you deliver to the offer.

Commission rate. This will show how much in percent you will get out of each sale made.

Refund rate. This is one that's overlooked but it important as it determines how satisfied customers are after their purchase. A low refund percentage will likely mean more commissions kept in your pocket.

ClickBank

In clickbank.com, click on the Marketplace link.

Now choose a category:

For this example, I'm going to choose *e-business & e-marketing*.

Here's what to look for:

MARKETPLACE
Choose from thousands of great prod

CLICKBANK

GIFT INSIDE

Advertisement

Resources

Recently Removed

Categories

▸ ARTS & ENTERTAINMENT

▸ BETTING SYSTEMS

▸ BUSINESS / INVESTING

▸ COMPUTERS / INTERNET

▸ COOKING, FOOD & WINE

▸ E-BUSINESS & E-MARKETING

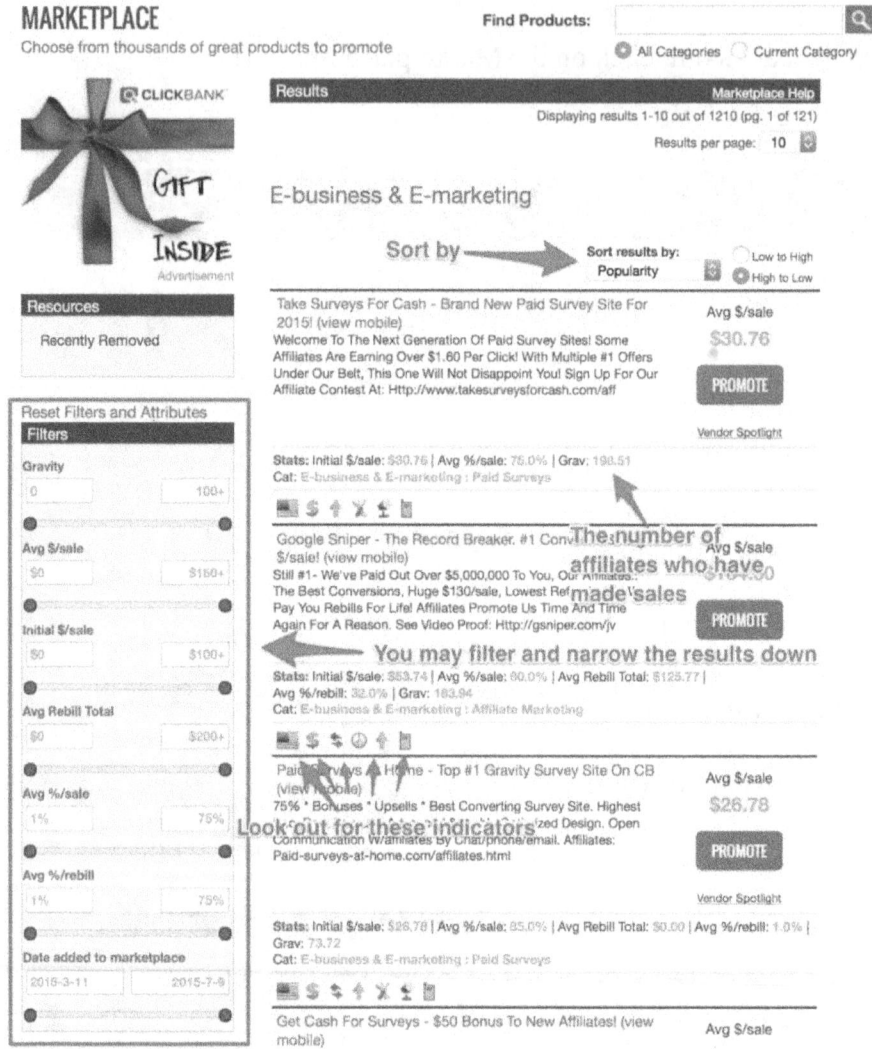

For the ClickBank Marketplace, the main measurement you want to look for is the Gravity. The gravity indicates how many distinct affiliates have made sales in the past 12 weeks.

For more information about ClickBank Gravity, go here: http://www.cbgraph.com/articles/clickbank-gravity.html

You may also want to check out the indicators and features below its listing. You'll find the following the language, whether it's one-time billing or recurring, whether the vendor provides affiliate promotional tools and many more.

That is the technical part of looking for good offers to promote. With this knowledge, you should be able to confidently determine whether a product is worth promoting or not on any affiliate network.

A few other things you want to make sure you do:

Your Opinion

Another important tip is to pick something that you care about and that you're exited for. This is a good idea because you'll find it's much easier to sell something that you *genuinely* believe is an amazing product. If your item is something you feel is trashy or a waste of time and money, then you can bet that your sales pitch is going to lack the oomph that it needs.

Go With What Works

That said, you also want to avoid being too obscure or taking too much of a gamble. The point is, that there are some very rich marketers online who have gotten rich selling specific products – and you have the option to sell those *very same* products! For this reason, it doesn't really make much sense to sell anything else.

Is it exciting, original or daring? No – but it's proven to work and it's straightforward. Sometimes that's all you need, especially when you're just starting out. That doesn't mean that you can't still pick something in your niche that you really like though – just find the best selling examples in that bracket and then try selling them yourself.

Is it Desirable?

If you're not sure how a product is performing, or you don't know whether you can replicate the success you've seen others enjoy, then you should ask yourself just generally whether you think it's something that has good potential for sales. Or more simply still: would *you* buy it?

We'll get onto selling later and how to go about making someone really want your product… But briefly one of the most important tips is to focus on the emotional hook and the 'value proposition'. In other words, how will you make people really want this item? What is it that it will do for them?

This is why making money products are so effective as well as dating e-books – they offer you a very concrete and significant lifestyle change/upgrade. What you should be looking for is things that appear to offer 'the answer'.

The Profit

Of course another thing to think about is the potential profit you could earn from the product and from each sale. I explained in detail on stats and numbers to look out for earlier.

This is what makes selling a service or a membership so appealing – because if you look at your commission over that customer's lifetime, you can stand to earn thousands.

For a single product meanwhile, you might want to compare which ones you can sell for more and which ones offer you 40% versus 60%. Now think about the volume you're likely to sell – you'll sell a lot more books than desktop computers so even if the profit is higher per unit, that doesn't necessarily make it the best pick.

Free Materials

Some affiliate products you find online will be so desperate to encourage sales that they're willing to give away extra materials to help you sell. Sometimes you'll be given the text for landing pages for instance and whole web designs. Some sites will even package their affiliate offers as being get rich quick schemes and products in themselves.

Be very cynical when assessing the added value these offer (it's always worth asking why they're so desperate to get more sellers) but at the same time, it is worth considering the added value that such extras represent.

And the *best* types of free materials that those that can help you to provide more value to your customers. For instance, some sellers will give you things like free 'reports' that you can use to incentivize a purchase.

What's the Market Like?

We've already looked at target demographics and markets in the context of subject and niche but there are other considerations to take here too. For instance, you need to ask what the people buying your product are *like* and how much else there is available for them to buy.

So if you're selling an e-book on making money online, you will largely be selling to: entrepreneurs and middle managers who want out of their current jobs. This is a very good audience because they have disposable income and are generally impulsive. You also have the added benefit here of selling something that they'll profit from, meaning they can earn back the money that they spent.

Additionally, this audience provides you with a very clear 'route to market'. That is to say, there are some very clear ways you can reach them – through forums, at conferences and via certain websites. On the downside? This market, as mentioned, is also saturated. We've all seen countless sales pages selling e-books about making money online and thus we've become rather cynical.

So what about another product? Well, if you had an e-book on making money from arts and crafts for instance, you could have an entirely different market. Now you might be targeting creative students, housewives and the elderly. These markets may have less disposable income but they're also far less commonly marketed too *and* they have some clear routes to market.

You can do a lot of guess work when it comes to choosing which market is best for your product. Generally though, the better strategy is to actually *research* the market first. That means taking a look at the existing products on the market, checking out some websites in that niche, signing up for some e-mail newsletters in that niche and reading the statistics. You'll likely find that you can learn a lot about each niche and which is best for you to enter into.

So that's quite a lot to consider and it might seem quite daunting. Don't worry too much though: to start with a very safe strategy is to try selling a product that is in your niche and that you can see other sellers have had a lot of success with.

How To Get Your Referral/Affiliate Link For a Product

By now, you should already have a list of potential products you would like to promote.

The next step is to get your referral link.

In ClickBank, you can simply click on the Promote button, enter your ClickBank Account Nickname and optionally a Tracking ID (if you want to track where the sale came from) and you will be given your affiliate link.

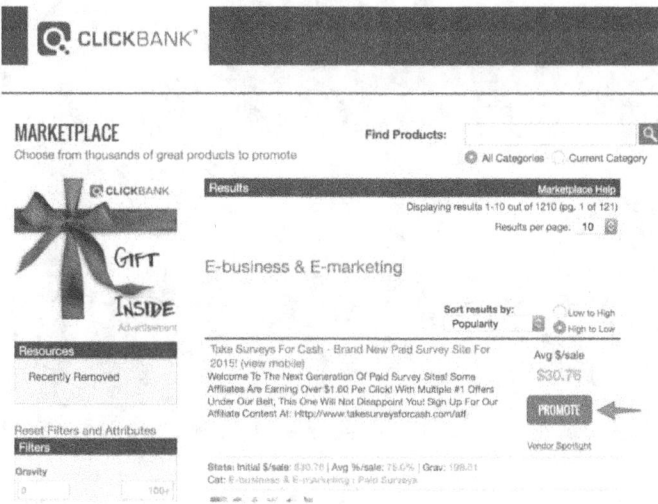

In JVZoo, make sure you are logged in and then simply click the Get Links button:

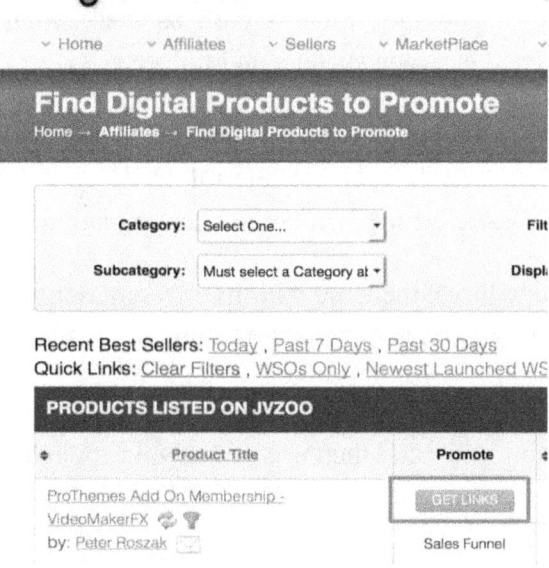

How To Build a Landing Page To Promote Offers as an Affiliate

At this point in the book you should now have a good working understanding of affiliate marketing and how it works. At the same time, you should also have some ideas regarding how you're going to find your product and how you're going to choose the right one. Make sure to spend time on this part, as that's what will really make the difference between success and failure.

Now though, you need to take the next step which is actually selling the product. You have your referral URL and your account with your seller/JVZoo/Amazon... so how do you begin generating money for it?

As we will see, there are various different options and each has different advantages and is more or less suited to different types of product.

One of the most common and most popular methods though is to build a landing page and then use this as your main 'tool' for landing sales.

What is a Landing Page?

Landing pages are also sometimes known as 'sales pages' or 'squeeze pages'. Their role is essentially to offer you a single point from where you can convert your visitors into buyers.

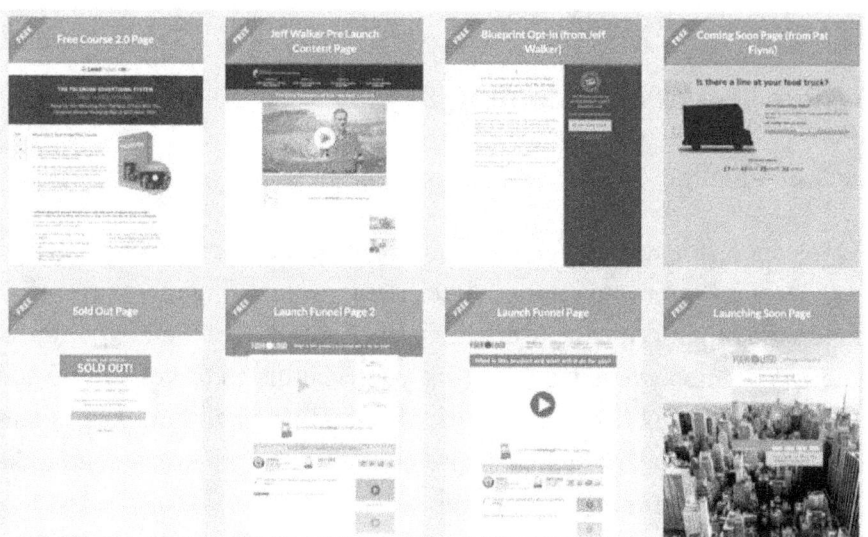

This is different from an e-commerce store because it's not a 'shop'. Rather, it's a page of text or images that all promote *one* single product. The text meanwhile is going to be entirely 'sales' oriented and with the sole goal of converting visitors and making the product sound amazing. This will be interspersed with 'Buy Now' buttons, which will contain your referral link.

Over time, you will tweak and add to your landing page and this will let you create something that is optimized in its ability to make sales. Eventually, what you'll be left with is a single destination that gives you the best shot at turning visitors into buyers. You can then focus your marketing efforts on getting people *to* that landing page.

The idea of using a landing page is to "pre-sell" your customers or in other words warm up your visitors so that by the time they land on the actual product being promote, they already know what to expect.

And they also tend to have some specific tropes that set them apart from more general web design...

Design Tropes of a Landing Page

Lack of Chrome

For instance, a landing page will usually have no other 'chrome' on it at all. Chrome refers to things like borders and menus that break immersion but provide the user with more control over their experience. Whereas on most websites you *want* your visitors to travel around and see different pages though, the aim of a landing page is to keep them *right where they are*. Thus, there are no menus, no adverts and no links – all there is the text and the images.

The *only* link that can take someone away from your landing page will be the 'Buy Now' button. They can leave the site by clicking back or closing the tab of course but even that will often result in a pop-up window asking if they're sure they want to leave!

Thin, Narrow Design

Another common design trope of landing pages is to be long, thin and narrow. The idea is that the visitors will be hooked by your text as soon as they land on your page and from here they'll then have to scroll gradually through the site.

The reasoning for this type of design is that it is more effective at immersing your visitors in your text and getting them committed to buying. As they scroll further and further down the page, they will feel as though they're investing more of their time and effort into learning about your product. The theory then goes, that they'll ultimately want to click 'buy' at the end because otherwise they'll feel as though they've wasted their time!

Narrow text is also eminently readable as it breaks it up and prevents it from being too dense. What's more, our eyes will naturally want to flit to the next line when they get to the end of an unfinished sentence.

Finally, the narrow design of a website also means that your audience gets taken further and further away from the top of the page – which on a mobile will make it harder for them to leave depending on the browser they're using!

Color Scheme

Colors can make a difference. Commonly, the color scheme of a landing page will be either red or orange largely. The reason for this is that this color has been shown to make us more impulsive. Simply seeing the color red has been shown to make people more impulsive and to raise their heartrate – as a result your audience will be significantly more inclined to click buy and to keep reading through the site. On the other hand, blue can symbolize trust and honesty.

Positioning

Where should you put your 'buy now' button? Think it doesn't matter?

The rule is actually quite strict: other than being interlaced throughout the website, the buy now button should go at the bottom and on the far right. This is what's known as the 'terminal point' because it's the last point that your eyes will reach when you're reading through the page.

Positioning your button thus is important because it means that after they've read all your sales patter, they'll then end up right on the buy button, rather than having to track around for it or read backwards.

If you take a look at landing pages online, then you should find plenty of examples and if you mimic that style, you'll be good to go.

Creating a Landing Page

The most important part of a landing page is actually the text. We're not going to discuss that here though, as persuasive writing is a general skill that applies to a number of different aspects of your affiliate marketing strategy. We'll come to that later…

Right now then, we'll focus on how you can go about creating the landing page you're going to sell from. The good news is that the nature of landing pages makes them easy to create. There are no menus, no animations and no fancy layouts – just a long, narrow tower of text and images.

The fastest and easiest way to create a landing page is to use LeadPages (http://leadpages.net).

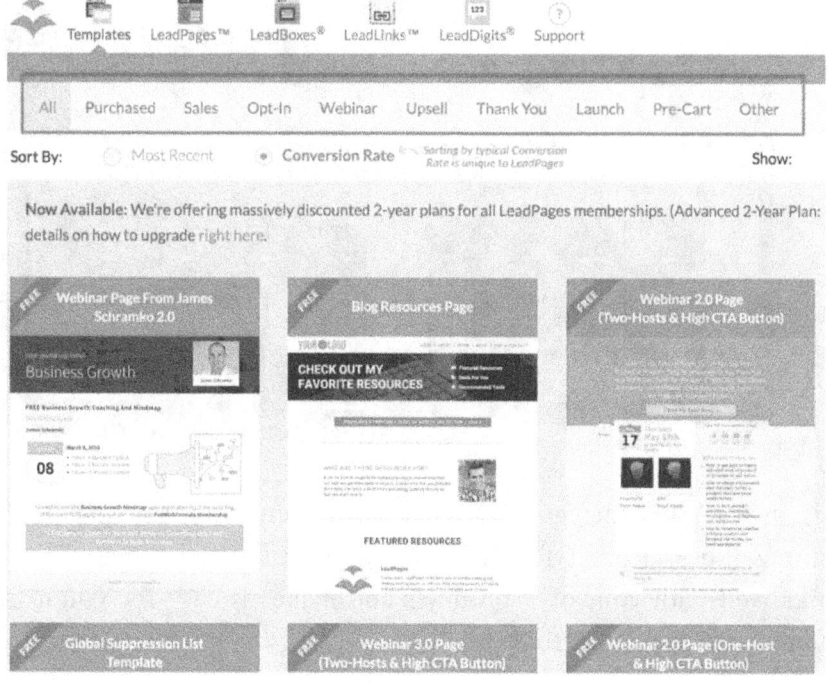

With LeadPages, you can create a landing page in a snap. It's all drag-and-drop functionality and there's zero coding required.

To create this in HTML and CSS then is actually very simple and it doesn't really require an expert designer. That said, if you want to automate the process even more and ensure that the result is something that looks professional and is almost guaranteed to convert, then a good choice is to use a tool designed specifically to help you build landing pages.

If you have a WordPress site, then you can do this fairly easily through a number of plugins aimed specifically at digital marketers. There are also themes that are designed to work as landing pages.

Another great option is to use OptimizePress (http://optimizepress.com), which for many marketers has become essentially the industry standard.

33

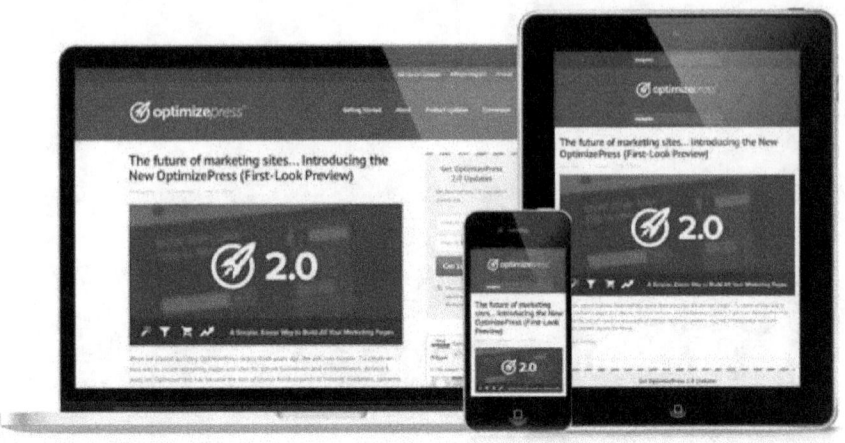

This is a tool for quickly and easily creating landing pages. OptimizePress is great for affiliate marketers but as a bonus it also works well with your own products and makes it easy for you to add payment options and delivery.

Split Testing

The idea of a landing page is that *everything* geared up to helping you make the maximum possible sales. This means everything from the text, to the layout, to the graphics, to the price.

Unfortunately, you're unlikely to get this right first go. Unless you're a highly experienced internet marketer, you probably need to hone your skills somewhat. Fortunately, there's a perfect way to do this which is with a process called 'split testing'. Here, you publish two slightly different versions of the same website with just a minor tweak. From there, you can then see which performs the best and which generates most sales. After getting enough traffic to make a relatively confident conclusion, you either keep or abandon that change based on sales. This is effectively natural selection and it allows you to evolve your site to the point where it's 100% optimized for selling your product to your audience.

34

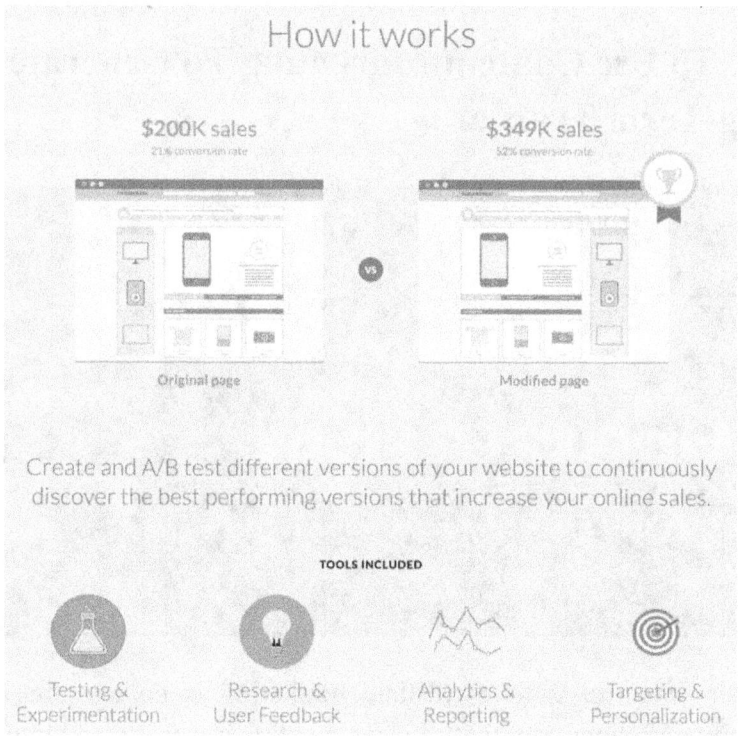

The sorts of changes and tweaks you can experiment with vary but they include alterations to the text, the headers, the color schemes and more. You can automate this with a number of WordPress plugins, one of the best is Optimizely (https://www.optimizely.com/) and Visual Website Optimizer (https://vwo.com/).

How To Use Content Marketing To Generate Long-Term Traffic

Another powerful tool in affiliate marketing is content marketing. Content marketing essentially means creating a website or blog, rising in prominence and then using that in order to sell your product.

The great thing about content marketing is that it works so well in tandem with numerous other sales techniques. In particular, content marketing is highly compatible with having a landing page and in fact, often the objective of content marketing will be to send people to your landing page.

Content marketing's broader objective though is to make you into a trusted expert in your niche. In the business, this is referred to as being a 'thought leader' or an 'authority'. This way, when you then recommend a product, people will be more likely to listen to you and to buy the product you suggest.

So how do you go about using content marketing?

How To Get Started With Content Marketing

To start with, you will need a blog and that will be where you will publish your posts and let people know about your business. At the same time, you can then combine this with a strong social media presence, heavy branding and maybe even a YouTube channel, such that your audience can get to know you.

Be successful at this is largely about posting regularly and offering *real* value to your readers. Don't try and sell right away but instead spend your time building up trust and respect in your niche. Every time you publish a blog post, you should ask yourself: is this something you would read? Is it comprehensive, engaging and unique enough to stand out from all the other posts in this niche? Does it make you look like you really know your stuff?

Spend time designing your logo and website and then work to ensure you are creating a consistent vision that will help you to establish yourself on the net.

This might all sound like a lot of work and you might find the idea of becoming a thought leader to be nerve wracking. However it is *very* much worth it. The main reason for this, is that when you are an authority in your niche, you will not only be able to sell the one product – but really *any* product that you subsequently want to. You'll have a direct 'route to market' letting you directly reach thousands of buyers and they will always be happy and willing to take your advice.

This is the strategy that most affiliate marketers will use to become truly wealthy but it does take a little longer. Note as well that if you're going to use this strategy, you do need to think carefully about the quality of the products you recommend. If you promote a very substandard product too forcefully you will lose the respect of your buyers and ultimately they'll; be less likely to consider your future recommendations.

Promoting Your Blog

Running a highly successful blog is essentially a license to print money but getting there is a long road. This is not a case of 'build it and they will come' – but rather something you need to work hard at if you're going to be successful.

Even if you post the best quality content to your blog in the world on a regular basis, if no one knows it's there, then it's not going to provide you with much benefit.

So how do you get the word out?

Social Media

One option is to use social media and social bookmarking sites. Over time, you can use social media synergy in order to build up a large following and in future you'll be able to use that to instantly reach a huge selection of people.

In the short term though, to get those initial viewers it makes a lot of sense to use social bookmarking sites. These are sites like Reddit and like Digg where people share their favourite sites. You can also try posting to Google+ communities.

The reason this is so effective is that it allows you to communicate to a captive audience, all of whom have a shared interest in your specific subject. Thus, you can gain a massive amount of shares and reads almost immediately as long as the title of your blog post is enticing enough.

Head to the Reddit fitness page (reddit.com/r/fitness) and post an article on 'How to Get Great Abs' and you'll get 'downvoted' to a bad extent.

On the other hand though, if you post something that sounds more unique and more interested 'New Study on the Best Training for Superhuman Strength' and you can potentially get thousands of views overnight. If you've then incorporate your social media into your page, this can in turn help you to build a large amount Twitter followers, Facebook 'likes', YouTube subscribers *etc*.

Influencer Marketing

Influencer marketing is another form of social media marketing that is incredibly effective when used correctly. Essentially, this type of marketing allows you to leapfrog the competition and get much more quickly to a point where you're reaching a much larger audience and influencing them all the more.

How does this work? Simple: by taking advantage of the ground work that other marketers have already done. Influencer marketing means finding someone in your niche who already has a lot of influence (an *influencer*) and then contacting them and requesting that they broadcast a message on your behalf. You might pay them to do this, you might create content specifically designed for them to share, or you might agree to do each other the same favour and thereby share your existing audiences. This technique can be immensely powerful when used correctly.

SEO

At the same time, you should also be using SEO to try and further your efforts in promoting yourself online. SEO stands for 'Search Engine Optimization' and it essentially means managing your content, your website and your marketing in such a way that it will enhance your site's visibility on Google.

In the past, SEO was very simple and all it really entailed was creating lots of content with your 'keywords ' (the search terms) in it and generating as many links to your website as possible (with the keywords as your anchor text).

Over time though, Google has evolved and has become much smarter. A lot of internet marketers were using SEO to manipulate their position on Google and this resulted in Google having to update its algorithms. Now Google is sensitive to anything that looks like obvious SEO and instead the only way to climb the ranks of the search engine reliably is to update your site regularly with high quality content and to use natural language. At the same time, you still want to gather inbound links, but they should be a wide range of varied different links from different sources and that are written differently.

As such, content marketing and SEO are largely inseparable these days. Good content marketing *and* good SEO involve populating your site with lots of very high quality posts. At the same time, if you do this well, it will encourage people to share your content and link to it of their own free will. Great quality content that encourages sharing is what's called 'link bait'.

Guest Posting

One more strategy that still works well for SEO – as long as you don't overdo it – is guest posting. Guest posting essentially means that you are writing a post for a blog other than your own and offering them to publish it free of charge. As a result, they get more content for their site and this helps them to provide their visitors with more value. But of course you aren't just doing this out of the good of your heart, as in exchange you ask them to include a link back to your website along with some description about who you are (called an author box). This way, they get free content and you get a link from a well-known blog and an authority.

E-Mail Marketing

E-Mail marketing can be used as a supplement to content marketing, as a separate endeavour or as a bit of both. Of course the whole idea behind e-mail marketing is to create a mailing list of people who have shared their email with you because they want to hear about your products, services and deals. From there, you can then provide them with newsletters and value directly in their inboxes, or you can sell to them by promoting your best products and services as an affiliate. The links will work the exact same way directly through e-mails (and JVZoo is even optimized for this) and the process either way is a very personal and direct way to influence your audience.

The first step in e-mail marketing then is to build that audience. Interestingly, you can do this in the very same ways you might get sales for an affiliate product (and in that way it might appear to be somewhat a step removed from this more direct form of marketing). For instance, a landing page can be geared up to generate e-mails and leads and this is when it's normally called a 'squeeze page'. Likewise, you can add sign-up forms, also called 'opt-in forms' right into your blog posts, on your home page or in your right hand column as a widget. However you go about this, just make sure that your mailing list is prominent and that you're effectively communicating why it is that your audience should listen to you and enter their e-mail address. In other words: how are you offering value.

You can also aid this process by incentivizing your audience to sign up. You can do this for instance by giving away a free e-book, or a free discount for your product. Either way, this means that they get more value simply by providing their e-mail address which many people will view as a good deal!

Setting Up An Autoresponder

In order to make your mailing list work, you need to be able to manage people subscribing and unsubscribing and you need to be able to verify e-mails, store them all, back them up and generally do a lot of management. This is where an 'autoresponder' comes in, which is essentially a tool designed specifically for this purpose.

Autoresonders are unfortunately not free and that means you need to pick which one you're going to use carefully. As with affiliate networks, there are three big choices that people tend to pick from when they select autoresponders and these are: MailChimp, AWeber and GetResponse. There are others but these three are the ones you will hear about most often and that generally have the most support in terms of WordPress plugins etc. I have used all three and believe GetResponse is the best:

http://pureresiduals.com/getresponse

Working out which of these options is the most cost effective isn't as simple as comparing a flat rate as the amount you pay will depend on how many subscribers you have. But, again, feature-wise and for scalability, GetResponse is number 1. And, believe me, you don't want to move your records to them later! I made that costly mistake.

Free Trial:

GetResponse:

Subscribers	Monthly Fee
1,000	$15
2,500	$25
5,000	$45
10,000	$65
25,000	$145
50,000	$250
100,000	$450

Try to think ahead – just because one option is the cheapest now, it might come back to haunt you if you end up with a lot of subscribers (which of course is the objective!).

E-Mailing

Again, we're going to get into persuasive writing in a bit but just note that when using e-mail marketing to sell an affiliate product it pays to take a more gradual approach. In other words, don't make your first message something that's trying to sell a product. Instead, use a 'sequence' where you start by providing value and generating trust (to get them to open future e-mails), then move on to talking about your 'upcoming amazing deal' and then eventually provide the link.

The more you generate buzz and excitement around your product, the more likely you'll be to get sales.

How To Use Persuasive Writing To Make More Sales

Now onto the best bit: persuasive writing. For content marketing, sales pages and e-mail marketing, persuasive writing is an absolute must and when you get it right, you'll be able to sell like a *Jedi*.

Here we will go over some of the tenants of good persuasive writing.

Grabbing Attention

Your first goal with persuasive writing is to grab attention. This is actually a big challenge these days on the web, seeing as everyone is in such a hurry and is so used to being overstimulated by adverts, sales scripts, movies and more.

In other words, there are a million and one things vying for our attention at any given time and for anything in particular to stand out it needs to work hard.

This is why a good way to start you sales script is with a short statement, ideally something bold or maybe a question to the audience. When you do this, your audience will immediately be pulled in. Another strategy is to leverage the curiosity of the audience – start your script with something unusual so people are surprised and keen to read on to see where you're going with it.

What you mustn't do is start with a long waffling introduction. Think: 'BAM I'm here!' and then let the rest follow.

Use Questions

Why are questions a good way to win over your audience? Mainly because they're naturally engaging. When we read a rhetorical question, it doesn't only feel as though someone is talking directly to us but it also forces us to stop and reflect on what's being said. This way we are now engaged with the information, rather than just passively taking it in.

Use Short Statements and Paragraphs

Just as you want to start with a short, abrupt statement, you should also aim to do this throughout the rest of your text.

And then move on to the next line.

Why?

Because it adds to the drama of what you're saying.

But better yet?

It encourages your audience to keep scrolling down!

In general, you want to avoid any long paragraphs which only have the effect of putting your audience off. Bear in mind that most of us don't read thoroughly anymore – we tend instead to simply 'skim read' and you need to organize your text in such a way that this can work well.

Use Headers

Also conducive to skim reading is the use of headers. Headers are important because they let us jump to particular sections in the text. When used correctly, your headers should *alone* provide the whole story *and* sufficient incentive for your audience to want to buy your products.

Have a Narrative

Another way to engage your audience and to ensure they don't leave before they've reached the end of the page is to use a narrative thread throughout. In other words, your text be based around a story from your perspective (first person).

So if you're trying to sell a book on making money online, you might start with the sentence:

'Only a few months ago I was really struggling with money'

Or maybe:

'Want to know how I just made $1,000 overnight?'

This works for a number of reasons. For starters, it allows us to imagine ourselves in the narrator's shoes which increases the 'desire factor'. At the same time, this strategy also makes it very hard to stop reading. That's because we almost always want to finish stories to find out what will happen – we've evolved to listen to stories and to wait until the end of the narrative and this can be used to the seller's advantage. Even if they're not interested in what you have to say, they might want to know how the story ends!

Fears

Using the narrative first person allows your readers to step into your shoes and makes you relatable. This is a great start. One thing you then want to do with that, is to voice their concerns and allay any fears they might have.

So in the case of a 'get abs tomorrow' diet, the fear is of course that the diet is dangerous or that it's a fad. You can put these concerns to rest with the first person narrative by saying:

'Of course I was worried this was just another scam like all the rest – maybe even dangerous – but nope, this time things were different!'

Think of the Value Proposition

Most important of all though is to think of your 'value proposition'. This is basically where the value lies in what you're selling – how your product or service will tangibly improve the life of the person buying it.

The old saying goes that you sell 'warm heads' rather than hats. In other word, the reader only cares about how the product benefits them.

And when you outline this, you want to really go for the feels. In other words, get them to really visualize their life after your product. If it's a product that will make them money, then get them to imagine all the trappings of that lifestyle: travel, boys toys, big houses, yachts, private planes... you name it!

Think: AIDA

As for your basic structure, your first objective is to ensure that your audience knows what it is you're selling. Remember, they likely won't have heard of your product before – so don't leap straight into the pitch.

'AIDA' stands for 'Awareness, Interest, Desire, Action' and is a good outline for the flow of your sales pitch.

Use Authority and Social Cues

You can encourage people to want to buy your products by combining authority sources and social cues. For instance, tell your audience that your product is backed by science (don't lie – find a study!), find a trust worthy testimonial and get testimony from previous customers. You have a very clear ulterior motive – so let them hear from someone who doesn't!

Likeability

Throughout it all, try to make yourself as likeable as possible. Countless studies show us that the more likeable we are, the more able to persuade we are.

Add Time Pressure and Scarcity

If you've employed all these methods, then you should have a scenario where people are excited for your product and how it can help them to change their lives. But in order to seal the deal you need them to put their money where their mouth is and this is the hardest part.

The key now is to get your buyers to act on impulse and not to go away and 'think about' the proposal. *Most* of the purchase we make are done on impulse and based on emotion rather than logic. If they leave to think about it, they almost certainly *won't* come back. It's now or never, so you need to get them to act fast.

You can do this by using 'time pressure' and 'scarcity'. Time pressure means saying they have only X amount of time to buy your product and that is super effective because it simultaneously introduces scarcity –

meaning there are fewer versions of your product out there in the world. This is great because scarcity = value.

Direct Marketing – The Fast Way To Start Making Money as an Affiliate

All the strategies we've looked at so far focus on long-term plans to build trust and momentum and to eventually turn that into sales.

But what if you want to market directly and skip all the fluff? You won't build the same long-term business model but you'll make money *fast* and that's what a lot of people are keen to do. Remember as well that you can combine any of the techniques in this book. So you can use a blog and content marketing to gain trust *and* you can use direct marketing to make shorter-term income.

Direct marketing basically means using your link and showing it directly to your audience. There are a number of ways you can do this:

Paid Advertising

The most obvious way to get your link out there *immediately* is with advertising. The best option here will be to use a form of PPC advertising, which means 'Pay Per Click'. With this type of advertising you only pay when someone actually clicks on your ads. This amount is predefined by 'bidding' on advertising space and by setting an advertising budget.

As a general rule though, you'll usually only pay a few cents or a few dollars at most for each click. This then means that if you're getting $30 per sale on your affiliate product, you'll be able to make a lot of 'mistakes' before you stop breaking even. In general you can have less than a 2.5% success rate and still make a profit.

What's more, if you use your advertising platforms correctly, you can target your audience and thereby ensure that you're only advertising to people who are likely to want to buy your product.

With Facebook Ads for instance, you can target your audience based on their age, sex, location, marital status, job description and even hobbies. That means you can make sure that your fitness e-book ad only gets seen to be people who are young, male and who list 'fitness' as their hobby. Likewise, you can ensure that it's managers who see your advert for an SEO e-book aimed at small business.

With Google AdWords on the other hand, you can target by search term and this effectively allows you to get the same benefits as SEO – but immediately and without any chance of it not working. So for example, you can use AdWords to target the search term 'e-book on making money online'. Remember, you won't get charged if no one clicks!

As a quick tip, consider placing the price of the affiliate product right in the title of the advert. This way people won't click unless they're at least *theoretically* willing to spend some money on whatever it is you're selling.

More Direct Marketing Techniques

There are a ton of other ways you can start making money immediately from direct marketing though too.

One example is to sponsor a big blogger or social media influencer to use your link. Another is to provide guest posts with your affiliate link embedded in them, or a link to a landing page – this way there's zero up-front investment so you'll be making pure profit. This is another form of influencer marketing.

You can also post directly onto forums, answer questions on sites like Quora, or post to social bookmarking sites – just be careful not to get banned. You can create a YouTube video and get a surprising number of views without having to do any marketing or legwork and you can even hand out fliers and leaflets in person containing your affiliate link or landing page.

Another trick is to give out free e-books. If your e-book provides real genuine value to your audience but is filled with affiliate links, then this can be a great strategy. Think about it: if someone e-mailed you an e-book about building biceps completely for free, you'd probably at least look at it. And if it highly recommended a product, then *some* people would click on the link. If you're adventurous you can even use Kindle to do this – giving away an e-book for free via Amazon and incorporating your affiliate links that way.

Advanced Affiliate Marketing Techniques And Lessons

How To Win Affiliate Contests

Sometimes product creators will want to encourage a little extra effort in their affiliates to get them to push their products even harder. This is especially common if they are launching the product for a limited time only such as a 7 day special. They then offer cash prizes for the affiliates that bring in the most money, offering yet more incentive to this particular form of incentive advertising.

This snapshot was taken from a product creator's affiliate contest which shows the prizes affiliates could potentially win:

1st Place: $500

2nd Place: $250

3rd Place: $100

4th Place: $50

5th-10th Place: $25

57

This particular example shows that 'No Minimum'. This means that no minimum sales are required to qualify for the cash prizes. However, you will find other product owners' contests to have a minimum sales required. A minimum is used as a safety guard in case their launch does not reach the amount of sales expected.

So how do you go about winning a contest in order to win the prizes?

Basically, now you have to think that you are not only trying to sell, you're also trying to *compete*. That means you need to find a way to offer something extra on top of what everyone else is offering. Try incentivizing purchases by offering bonuses to buyers – free e-books for instance, discounts off of future products, videos… anything you can think of! The best way to go about it is to offer bonuses that are highly related to the product being sold. For instance, if you are promoting a product related to burning belly fat, you could offer bonuses such as eBooks on how to get six pack abs. Another example – if you are promoting a membership plug-in, you could offer video tutorials on how to get started using the plug-in.

Here's a real-life example of just one bonus offered when customers purchase a course called 'Healthy Business, Healthy Life':

BONUS #4

LOSE THE BELLY FAT - Full PLR!

*50 Simple Ways To Lose Weight
Without Yo-Yo Dieting*

Includes:

- **100% Full private label rights**
- High quality eBook
- Professionally-designed graphics
- Done-for-you Opt-in page
- Ready-made Salesletter
- Start reselling it for 100% profit!

Valued at $27.00!

As you can see, this bonus eBook is highly related to the main product being promote – Healthy Business, Healthy Life.

Offering bonuses not only separates yourself from other affiliates, but it also increases conversion rates since your customers will be more inclined to purchase.

Building your audience will also help you to get a head start on the competition this way. More leads in your email database always leads to more sales in the end, so always make it a priority to build your email database or as Internet marketers like to call it – "email list".

Look for these contests and opportunities as they *can* provide a good opportunity to make money and the buzz and competition will only push you to try harder and do better.

How to Transition From Affiliate Marketer To Product Creator

Note that there is another approach: which is to transition more gradually from the one business model to the next.

For instance, you can find an affiliate product you like the looks of, start making money from it with whatever marketing approach best suits you and then tweak this until it's optimized. Then, once you've got the income working 100%, you simply swap the product for your own product so that you start getting 100% of each sale.

Maintain Good Relationships With Product Owners

One of the best ways to make sure you get the best treatment as an affiliate is to build relationships with vendors and products owners. By doing so you're seen not just as a regular affiliate but as a loyal and trustworthy partner. The keyword here is **partner**.

As a result, it's not surprisingly that they will bump your commission rate higher than what they usually offer to regular affiliates. In essence, there's always room for negotiation for extra benefits by building good relationships with vendors.

The ways in which you can maintain good relationships:

- Subscribe to their affiliate/partner newsletter to find out if there are any special launches or promotions. You want to be the first to take action on it.

- Let the vendors know where and how you are promoting their product(s) as a way to showcase your ability and willingness to make sales.

- Request for promotional tools that are unique to you and you only. Typically, vendors offer ready-made promotional tools where hundreds of other affiliates are using, too. Vendors are usually more than happy to provide something more unique for you and your audience. This may include slight adjustments to banner ads, email copy, ad campaigns and more.

Conclusion And Plan of Action

So there you have it: a ton of different methods you can use to start making money from affiliate products. That's a lot of information to swallow though, so as a more direct guide, just try to follow these key points:

- Choose your product by very carefully considering the target audience, the state of the market and the potential 'routes to market' that you could advertise through.

- Think as well about the product that will offer you the most profit in the short and long term.

- If you have a channel already with a big audience, start selling through that.

- Otherwise, set up a way to start making direct and immediate profit: most likely this will be through Google or Facebook ads.

- Now at the same time, work on creating an audience for yourself – begin by creating a blog in the correct niche.

- Now use a combination of social media marketing, content marketing, video marketing, influencer marketing and more to build trust and authority in your niche.

- You should also take this opportunity to collect e-mails.

- Eventually you can start selling directly by recommending the products you've selected to your audience.

- Then try another product!

- If you're interested in going one step further, you can also take your existing products that are selling well and swap them with a product that you've actually created.

And there you have it! That's really all there is to it – you just need to know how to really persuade your audience and you need to stick at the process so that you fine-tune your approach. Eventually, you can be making BIG money while you sleep from products you didn't even create!

The Professional Website Secret

Turning Your Favorite Passion into a Thriving Business Absolutely
Free of Charge!

I noticed this online business opportunity years ago and disregarded it
due to a sign-up fee. But, that has since changed. You can now Learn
while you Earn, which is a fantastic change. (Check it out
http://pureresiduals.siterubix.com/wealthyaffiliate.) **Yep, no credit
card needed**. Wealthy Affiliate has been around for a decade and only
seems to get better.

There are so many other scams and wanna-be-legit programs out there.
I have literally spent over $7,500 over the past 12 years checking them
out and bringing my readers the best of the best. I have purchased just
about every software tool, eBook, PDF or service claiming to be "The
One". Some, actually made me some money, but mostly I lost. I can
say that I'm very impressed with what Wealthy Affiliate has to offer.

What is Wealthy Affiliate?

Well, first, let me tell you what it's not. Wealthy Affiliate (WA) is not
some get-rich quick scheme, MLM or pyramid. I'm not saying there

64

aren't decent MLM programs out there. I have met some serious six-figure earners in MLM. But, as you're likely aware, they are few and far between. They either had a huge following to begin with OR they are just incredibly motivated with above-average PR skills. WA is more of what YOU can do. That another enticing feature.

Now, as I mentioned, it's not a get-rich quick opportunity. It's a real-deal, learn how to build an online passive income business opportunity. If you think you'll sign-up and immediately make cash without zero effort on your part, please don't continue reading this.

Okay, glad you're still here! Let's talk about training and....

...learning how the average person can gain the knowledge (from people doing it) to create a successful residual income business online.

The "Boot-camp" training is phenomenal. It's the most basic "step-by-step" training I have yet to see online. Couple that will more than 500 training videos and LIVE support and what more can you ask for? Additionally, for absolutely nothing, you get two websites to begin earning commission – did I mention NO credit card required?

This is definitely one of the most outstanding differences between WA and other the other so-called "businesses" I have reviewed. WA doesn't advertise with hype and false promises. They are all about helping you build a strong foundation with training and knowledge – the "Learn while you Earn" philosophy. And, it's truly something anyone willing to learn can accomplish.

Pros:

- **Clear Plan of Action**

- **All levels of training – Beginner and Advanced**

- **Video training, Step-by-step Tutorials and Courses**

- **10,000's of community members**

- **13 Full, Interactive Classrooms with tasks to complete**

- **Live & Interactive Help from owners and expert members**

- **2 Free Easy-to-Build Websites (you will also learn what to do with these sites)**

- **State of the Art Hosting**

- **A strict spam free environment.**

- **No up-sells, ever. (except Premium, of course)**

- **$0 Membership. Yes, completely FREE!**

Cons:

- **Too much information that can be overwhelming**

- **Sometimes I catch myself spending too much time on Live Chat – it's addictive.**

- **Not allowed to advertise/sell within WA. (This should be a warning for spammers who want to join WA just so they could try to sell something)**

- **Starter membership at zero cost is great, but you do have to upgrade to premium in order to access advanced training**

Wealthy Affiliate Review – Who is WA Best Suited For?

Obviously, WA isn't going to be a good fit for everyone. Wealthy Affiliate is all about gaining knowledge, training, creating your first website and driving web traffic to it effectively (and, totally "white hat".)

So, the training is how to successfully build a professional online presence and market your business. There are no shortcuts.

But, is Wealthy Affiliate for you?

Do you fall into one of the following categories?

- **A person who wants to make an extra income to supplement their salary.**

- *Stay at home moms who have some free time and are willing to spend it in front of the computer.*

- **Students who want to make money to help them pay for their tuition, some college students built 6-figure businesses from their dorm, using Wealthy Affiliate.**

- *Business owners who want to get more visibility online.*

- **Retired people who have free time and want to supplement their pension.**

- *People who are fed up of 9-to-5 and want to start their own business. Many Wealthy Affiliate members have been able to quit their "day job" to do online marketing full time.*

As I indicated, WA is a solid foundation for anyone seeking to obtain smart passive income online and go about it the right way. This program will give you the knowledge and training to take whatever you're passionate about and build an online business around it to create recurring income. This is the epitome of what Pure Residuals was created for.

What Exactly Do You Get Inside?

Wealthy Affiliate only costs $47/month.

Update: Wealthy Affiliate is now FREE to join! (<u>Join now</u>)

	Starter	Premium
	For Newbies to Get Started Fast!	For Those Who are READY for Success!
	$0 Per Month	$47 Per Month
	Create a Starter Account!	Go Premium Today!
Live Support	First 7 Days	Unlimited
Personal Affiliate Blog	Yes	Yes
Private Messaging		Unlimited
Websites	2 Websites	Unlimited Websites
Website Security Package		Yes
Website Backup		Yes
Beginner Training Course	Yes	Yes
Affiliate Bootcamp Training	Phase 1	All Phases
Live Video Classes		Yes
Video Walk-Throughs	Yes	Yes
Keyword Research Tool	30 Searches	Unlimited Searches
Training Classrooms	2	12
Affiliate Program	Yes	2x Higher Payout
Earn While you Learn	Yes	Yes
1-on-1 Coaching	First 7 Days	Unlimited
Best For	Getting Started	Those Ready to Earn!

Wealthy Affiliate (as you can see above) only has two membership options. i recommend **joining for free**. Get in on the training, meet the helpful membership, begin building your first website and marketing. Earn some cash and see what you think. In my opinion, you'll come to love it as much as I do. Then, only when you're ready, you can upgrade to the Premium membership to gain higher commission and access to the other levels of training.

Getting Started – Level 1

Get Rolling!	Understanding How to Make Money Online
Choose a Niche	Building Your OWN Website
Setting Up Your Website	Getting Your Site Ready For SEO
Finding Content Ideas From Keywords	Understand Website Pages
Creating Quality Website Content	Congratulations – Your Next Steps

Get Your Entrepreneur Certification

What you get with your FREE Starter membership:

- Instant access to over 500 training modules

- 2 free websites along with free hosting

- Access to 3 classrooms

- Live support from the owners for the first 7 days and support from many experts inside WA!

- 30 keyword searches a month

- Phase 1 of the Boot camp course, teaching you how to build an authority website.

Put Your Credit Card Away and

Go to http://pureresiduals.com/wealthyaffiliate to claim!

Professional Website Secret

What you get with your Premium membership:

- Live Video Classes

- Instant access to over 500 training modules

- Unlimited free websites along with free hosting

- Website Backup and Website Security Package

- Access to all 12 classrooms

- Unlimited Live support from the owners and support from many experts inside WA!

- Unlimited keyword searches

- All phases of the Boot camp course

- 100% higher commissions.

- Private access to my support.

- … and a lot more!

What I feel most impressed with is the stellar support you get from LIVE from Kyle and Carson (founders) and all the other active and enthusiastic members along with the crystal clear step-by-step training. All other programs out there talk about it, but certainly fail to deliver leaving the members dizzy with information – when it is actually available. With WA, there is help available with every step you take and a kudos for every goal reached.

You can get very constructive criticism on your website, marketing strategies and tips on how to make them better. You're not left waddling around in the dark on how to begin or take it to the next level.

Turn Your Passion into a Residual Income Business

Choose an Interest	Build a Website	Get Rankings & Visitors	Earn Revenue
It can be anything you want	We make this easy!	Google, Bing, Yahoo, Facebook	Sell Stuff that People Want!

Wealthy affiliate had developed the most outstanding training for the beginner, intermediate or professional – enabling anyone to take what they love, build a web presence, market it effectively and monetize it to create passive online income.

The Proof:

First $1000 Day (Best Day Ever)

Blog by Jay Gumbs [Premium] ⬛ Last Updated on Oct 14, 2013

⭐ ⚙ ▾ ✎ Affiliate 💬 8 ✉ 0

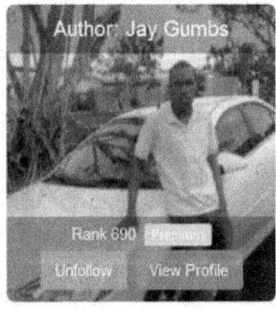

New Clickbank account. New niche. Record Day!

Period Ending	Sales
2008-05-16	$1,593.30
2008-05-01	$0.00
2008-04-16	$0.00

Daily Sales Subtotals

TBT - How I made $1000 in 3 days with Affiliate Marketing

Blog by Affilazon [Premium] Last Updated on Dec 05, 2014

⭐ ⚙ ▾ ✎ Affiliate 💬 9 ✉ 0

Throwback Thursday - yes I know it's Friday but I wanted to share a video I made a while back. Some of the information is slightly out of date but the principles still work. Take a look and enjoy. Please leave feedback if you have a chance. Here's the video link

Like This   12

TBT - How I made $1000 in 3 days with Affiliate Marketing

Blog by Affilazon `Premium` Last Updated on Dec 05, 2014

⭐ ⚙ ▾ 🔗 Affiliate 💬 9 ✉ 0

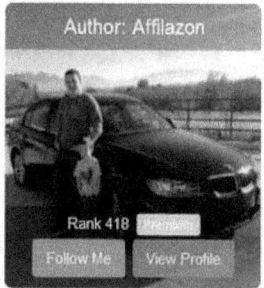
Author: Affilazon
Rank 418 `Premium`
Follow Me | View Profile

Throwback Thursday - yes I know it's Friday but I wanted to share a video I made a while back. Some of the information is slightly out of date but the principles still work. Take a look and enjoy. Please leave feedback if you have a chance. Here's the video link

Like This 12

Success! $292 Richer Today!

Blog by abigail11 `Premium` `Top 200` 🔲 Last Updated on Oct 09, 2014

⭐ ⚙ ▾ 🔗 Affiliate 💬 98 ✉ 0

Author: abigail11
Rank 112 `Premium`
Follow Me | View Profile

Hello dear WA friends. I have to say it is very exciting when logging into one of your affiliate accounts and seeing that you sold a product where you make 50% commission. I sold one product and made $198.50 in one hit and all together I sold $292.48 worth of products! **YES!!!** You see with the right attitude and commitment towards your goals, you can and will succeed.

I did it and it is exciting to see these results starting to show in just 5 to 6 months of dedicated work and sharing my passion from the heart.

I Quit! (My Job)

Blog by TJ7774 `Premium` Last Updated on Feb 10, 2014

⭐ ⚙ ▾ 🔗 Affiliate 💬 127 ✉ 0

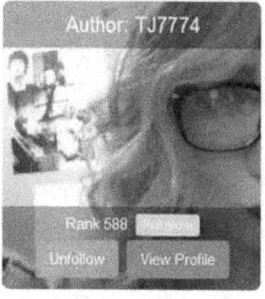
Author: TJ7774
Rank 588 `Premium`
Unfollow | View Profile

Today is the day- I am giving my notice at work!

Quitting is never an easy task for me to do. Any job I have had to quit in the past has always been hard. I would say quitting this job is about 10X harder than any as well. I love my supervisor and boss, my co-workers are great, and the people I get to see daily are awesome. Great pay and great benefits, so why would I leave such a secure and lovely job?

Frequently Asked Questions

I always get a ton of questions about my residual income businesses and how I make money online, so let me go ahead and provide some responses for the most frequent asked questions here. If you have any other questions I haven't covered, by all means, comment below or use my contact form.

Q: I am not very technical and I have never built a website. Will I still be able to create residual income with Wealthy Affiliate?

A: Definitely! If you're willing to learn and do what it takes to make it online, anyone can do this. The training is first rate and easy enough for beginners or pros alike.

Q: Do I have to promote Wealthy Affiliate to Make Money?

A: No, not at all! You don't have to sell a product or service or call anyone. You can simply use the training provided to build an online presence as instructed and totally market the products you wish – be it Amazon, eBay, Clickbank or Health Products. The choice is entirely up to you.

Q: I don't have a produt to sell. How can Wealthy Affiliate help me?

A: Wealthy Affiliate will teach you how to build a website and become a "Super Affiliate". An affiliate sells other people's products or services for a commission of the sale. The Bootcamp training will show you the very best online sources to find these products and services. If you need more on "What is Affiliate marketing" see my explanation here.

Q: Wealthy Affiliate is Free to join. What's the catch?

A: I can totally understand what you're saying. I said the same thing and was actually on the fence for over a year, before taking the plunge. I thought "there has to be some catch." But, I was wrong. I researched it on the best affiliate forums online and talked to other marketers I know and never was a bad word or negative comment given.

The Free Starter membership is upfront and exactly what they state. You can get inside and see the training and meet the members. Ask questions, build your website and Earn while you Learn. No credit card needed!

Q: If I build my websites with WA and then decide to leave, will I lose my websites?

A: No, even though the websites are built on state-of-the-art optimized servers, if you upgrade to Premium membership and ever decide to leave, you can take your websites (and all the content you created) with you.

Wealthy Affiliate Reviews – Negative Press?

As I mentioned, I have researched WA quite extensively – mostly before joining. There is nearly next to nothing online that has any negativity when it comes to WA. Wealthy Affiliate has been online for over a decade now and responsible for over 100,000 members.

Feel free to check it out for yourself. Do your due diligence and look around. But, I'm sure you'll discover the very same thing. *So, I urge you to join now and waste no more time!* I wish I had joined 10 years ago!

www.ingramcontent.com/pod-product-compliance
Lightning Source LLC
Chambersburg PA
CBHW070845180526
45168CB00002B/957